Balancing Your

Hormones

How Essential oils can help bring back the balance you've lost

By Eve Bell

Contents

Introduction

Whether you're a man or woman reading this, one thing is true. We all have hormones and they all fluctuate which leads to mood swings, sleeplessness, and other issues that we can live without. There is help and ways to bring your hormones back into balance. This book will help you:

- Explain what happens to our hormones as we get older.

- How to tell if you may be having hormonal issues

- What essential oils are good for which stages and disorders

- How to prepare the essential oils

- Foods that can help

- How to talk to your physician

- How to maintain level and balanced hormones

Both men and women have different symptoms and need different oils to help them during these transitional phases in life. This book will target both men and women. If you've even wondered how your emotions and general life back into sync, this is your book!

Chapter 1
Introducing your hormones

We all have them. We also have some we never thought we did. Did you know women have testosterone and men estrogen? It's true! We share the same hormones. In order to better get them in line, we have to know what they are and what they do.

In general, hormones are the messengers of our bodies, carrying instructions that range from sleep, hunger, fight or flight responses, and so much more. We have over fifty (50) hormones in our body, but we are only going to cover a small portion, and they are:

Melatonin: This hormone is an internal alarm for our bodies. It helps to regulate our sleep cycle and wakefulness. Our bodies produce more at night when it is time to sleep, and less as the night goes on to help us wake. Seasonal changes can sometimes affect how much melatonin our bodies make, which can contribute to Seasonal Affective Disorder (SAD). We also produce less as we age, leading to shorter sleep cycles or, in some cases no melatonin at all, which causes insomnia. This hormone is produced by the pineal gland.

Epinephrine: When you are scared, angry, nervous, or even working out, this hormone kicks in to provide you a boost. Also known as Adrenaline, this hormone can also elevate blood pressure and has been used in emergency rooms to jump start hearts, help asthmatics breathe and even stop the symptoms of a severe allergy attack. When your adrenal gland are not functioning normally, you are prone to manufacture less of this hormone, which will leave you chronically fatigued.

Norepinephrine: That feeling you get when your nervous or put in an extremely stressful situation. The rush of energy, the increased flow of blood, that's all this hormone's doing. It constricts the blood vessels to raise your blood pressure and also triggers the release of glucose to feed your muscles and give them the boost they need. This is the hormone that helps you deal with stress, and your adrenal glands make this one, too.

Cortisol: This is another and more widely known hormone for stress management. When your adrenals are working as they should, this hormone actually helps to burn fat during cardio and other exercise regimens. It is when you are having issues with your adrenal glands that there is a possibility that you may gain weight due to less cortisol being produced in your system.

Pregnenolone: This hormone is a building block to others. It helps to create, cortisone, testosterone, estrogen, progesterone. This is technically a steroid precursor, meaning it creates other natural steroids in the body. It is mainly manufactured by the adrenal gland, but it can be found in most of the other major organs as well. This hormone begins to wane as we get older. This can contribute to a low sex drive, mood swings, and so many other symptoms that are also found when you are lacking other hormones as well.

Testosterone: When we think of this, we think of men, burst of anger and also aggression, but that is only in cases where there is an overabundance of this hormone, and that is rare. In men, it helps to regulate their sex drive, energy levels, and it helps the body produce new cells and makes sure that males have strong bones and muscles.

When there is too much testosterone in the male body, it does contrubute to anger and temperment issues. A dip in this hormone in males means a lack of energy and desire in the bedroom.

A woman's ovaries produce testoterone as well as estrogen. Thought the amount of testosterone is lower than that of males, it is just as important for woment to have normal levels of this hormone. It keeps our reproductive systems working correctly, and helps to regulate our hair growth and other things, too. If it's to high, we have hair growth on our faces, a chance of balding and a lower voice. Our menstrual cycles stop when it's too high. When it's too low, it can contribute to a low libido and other problems.

Estrogen: Estrogen in males helps to balance out the testosterone. As men age, they produce less testoerone and more estrogen. A man's body can produce estrgen through fat cells. The more fat a male has, the more he can produce. This poses health risks like prostate cancer, diabetes and high lipids.

In women it oveshadows all other homones that regulate the reproductive system and affects a woman's mood, menstrual cycle, and also during pregnancy. It is the mainstay of the female hormonal system, but not having it in balance can mean changes in moods, hot flashes, night sweats, and the in the case of having too much in the system, cancer.

T3 and T4: These are hormones secreted by the thyoid to regulate your metabolism. When they are released, it increases heat in the body to burn fat and assimilate the nutrients you take in. When your thyriod starts to slow its activity, it can lead to weight gain, and also cancer. If your thyroid produces too much of these hormones, your metabolism is always in high gear and you can't keep weight on. Both conditions are highly dangerous.

Chapter 2
Essential Oils for the Endocrine System

That is simply a fancy name for all the glands in your body that produce the hormones you need to function. To get your hormones back into balance, you need to know which essential oils can help fortify which glands in this system. It is by creating synergistic (perfect) mixtures for the glands that we can start bringing the hormones back into balance by triggering them to produce the right amount of hormones needed.

In keeping with the list above, each list will provide essential oils to help trigger the hormone response. Not all essential oils can be used by everyone. Any shop that carries essential oils can walk you through a skin patch test to make sure that you won't have a reaction the essential oils. It is also advised that you discuss with your doctor what you are doing with the essential oils.

The system as a whole

There is a list of essential oils that can help the whole system. These are listed below:

Geranium Essential Oil (Pelargonium graveolens)

This oil is normally used for illnesses and support of the circulatory and nervous systems, but it has a calming effect on the system as a whole and helps the body's natural healing system by revitalizing tissue.

German Chamomile (Matricaria recutica)

This oil has been used for centuries for helping the body heal rapidly. It also clears the mind and relieves the body of stress. Chamomile, in general, has natural estrogen. This means it is beneficial in bringing hormones back into sync.

Myrtle Essential Oil (Myrtus communis)

This oil has undergone extensive research on its effects on the glandular system as a whole. It helps to regulate the production of hormones.

Nutmeg Essential Oil (Myristica fragrans)

This essential oil is another tonic the endocrine system. It helps to bring the system as a whole back into balance.

Sage Essential Oil (Salvia Officinalis)

Sage oil is beneficial in all aspects of both the oil and the herb itself. It helps to strengthen many systems including the endocrine system. It comes highly recommended for the pituitary and reproductive glands as well.

Spearmint Essential Oil (Mentha spicata)

This helps to boost the metabolism and stimulate the body as a whole.

Other things you can do.

The big thing to remember when bringing your hormones back into balance is to avoid the stress you can avoid and manage the stress you can't. Being in highly stressful situations a can lead to an abundance of cortisol in the system which leads to major health problems like heart disease.

Walk away from anything genetically modified and highly processed. All natural foods are best for your body. Use non-toxic cleaners for your body and your home. There are chemicals in household cleaners that can block endocrine function.

Chapter 3
The Pituitary

We're starting from the top. The Pituitary Gland is known as the Master Gland for the whole system. It manufactures hormones that regulate the functions of all the other glands in the system. It tells the thyroid when to produce more T3 and T4 to heat up the body and rev up the metabolism. When this gland is out of balance, it can cause the body to overproduce hormones that it doesn't need, leading to hyperthyroidism and other complications as well.

The essential oils listed above can reach the pituitary through inhalation or massaging into key spots in the skin. Here are a couple of recipes.

Bedtime Mixture

- 1 Tablespoon Sweet Almond or Apricot Kernel Oil

- 2 Drops of Sage

- 2 Drops of Geranium

- 2 Drops of German Chamomile

Mix all the ingredients together and then massage a small but into the base of the throat in front, at the base of the neck and the temples. Store the rest in an air-tight container.

Daytime Mixture

- 1 Tablespoon of Sweet Almond or Apricot Kernel Oil

- 2 Drops of Nutmeg

- 2 Drops of Spearmint

- 2 Drops of Sage

Mix all ingredients and massage into the same locations as above. You can apply this after you wake up in the morning and after lunch. The bedtime mix is for after dinner.

Mineral Salts

- 1/4 Cup Borax

- 1/4 Cup Baking Soda

- 1/2 Cup fine Sea Salt or ground steel cut oats

- 2 ounces of Sweet Almond oil or Apricot Kernel oil

- 5 Drops of Nutmeg

- 10 Drops Myrtle

- 5 Drops Spearmint

- 5 Drops German Chamomile

Mix the dry and wet ingredients separate. When both are completely mixed, mix the dry into the oils and make sure they are completely coated. Store in a tightly lidded container and allow sitting in a cool dark place overnight. When you're ready to use it, pour 1/4 cup into warm or slightly hot running water and soak yourself.

Evening Diffuser Mix

- 4 Drops German Chamomile

- 4 Drops Geranium'

- 2 Drops Sage

Mix all of them, and add them to a diffuser pad. If you do not have a diffuser, you can use a mug or candle warmer. The goal is to release the aroma into the air to trigger the limbic system of the brain which processes smell. Add all 10 drops to the surface before turning it on. Leave it on until you cannot smell it anymore. I mix like this should last about three hours.

Morning Diffuser Mix

- 2 Drops Nutmeg

- 2 Drops Spearmint

- 2 Drops Sage

- 4 Drops Myrtle

Mix all of them and add them as the diffuser recipe above. There are some essential oils that have a stimulating effect on the body, and this is why there are both day and night recipes. Most strong herbal essential oils, like Nutmeg, tend to act as stimulants, and should not be taken in any recipe before bed as they may cause problems when falling asleep.

Chapter 4
The Pineal Gland

If you have ever wondered how your body knows when it is day and then night starts to fall, thank your pineal gland. This little gland takes tryptophan and converts it into melatonin, which is essential for proper sleep rhythm. The problem is, as we age, this gland make less and less of it, leaving us with shorter sleep cycles and even insomnia. To target the pineal gland, we focus on essential oils that induce a relaxed state and allow our bodies to relax and our minds to rest.

Virginian Cedarwood oil
(Juniperus virginiana)

This essential oil can help to activate the pineal gland as well as relieve high strung nerves and other stress related sleeping disorders.

Frankincense Oil (Boswellia carteri)

This versatile oil is helpful to the pineal gland as well. It calms the nerves, sooths tempers and allows for a more relaxed state to help you sleep.

Sandalwood Oil (santolina chamaecyparissus)

This oil has been used for the treatment of insomnia and other nervous disorders as well. This is more pricey oil, and may not be budget friendly for most.

Lavender (lavandula angustafolia)

This is a staple in many aromatherapy cabinets. It has an affective calming effect on the nerves and the soothing aroma it presents can instantly calm someone who is having a hard time falling asleep.

Roman Chamomile (Chamaemelum nobile)

Another staple in the arsenal, this essential oil works hand-in-hand with the others to provide a soothing tonic to nerves, a relaxing feeling to the mind, and a slowing of the mind that lets the pineal gland activate and the melatonin flow.

Inhaling is the best a fastest way to activate this gland. A diffuser can be either a plug in diffuser or one that requires a tea light. You can pick one up at herb shops and some health stores. If you cannot find one, a mug warming plate works just as well. Add the oils before you plug in your method of choice.

Diffuser Blend

- 2 Drops of Frankincense oil

- 2 Drops Virginian Cedarwood oil

- 4 Drops of Lavender Oil

- 2 Drops of Roman Chamomile Oil

Mix all of the oils together and place them in the diffuser. This treatment can be left on all night, provided your delivery system is not a fire hazard.

Massage Oil

- 2 Ounces of Sweet Almond oil or Apricot Kernel Oil

- 5 Drops of Sage

- 5 Drops of Virginian Cedar

- 10 Drops of Lavender

- 5 Drops of Roman Chamomile

Mix all the ingredients together and place them in a dark glass jar. To use, rub a small amount into each temple and the base of the neck. This will allow the oils to trigger the gland.

Mineral Bath

- 1/4 cup borax

- 1/4 Baking Soda

- 1/2 cup coarse Sea Salt or ground steel cut oats (If you are hypertensive)

- 1/4 Cup Sweet Almond Oil or Apricot kernel Oil

- 10 Drops of Virginian Cedarwood

- 5 Drops of Lavender

- 5 Drops of Geranium

- 5 Drops of Roman Chamomile

Mix all the dry ingredients together. Mix all the oils together. Mix the dry into the oils and make sure they are well coated. Place it in a tightly lidded container and let it sit overnight. Use 1/4 Cup in warm running water.

This is just the start. In order to fully get the pineal gland in fine running order, don't forget to **add iodine-rich foods** to the diet such as kale, kelp, collards, cranberries, green beans, dark leafy greens, bananas, shrimp, and lobster. Skip the cocoa and go for the unprocessed cacao.

Foods with **tryptophan**, such as Turkey, will help the body manufacture melatonin.

Avoid Fluoride by using a filter that removes it, and also switching to toothpaste that does not contain any fluoride. This will drastically lower your fluoride intake, and you never really needed it for cleaner teeth anyway.

Add the **Apple Cider Vinegar**. Put a tablespoon of it in an eight ounce glass of water with lemon juice and honey. This will cleanse your system.

Make the switch to **Coconut oil**. Taking a teaspoon of this will help clean your system, and help with numerous other health issues as well.

Barley Grass and **Parsley** help to remove heavy metals from the system that can stop the pineal gland from working properly.

If you need a little extra help, you can mix lavender, chamomile and peppermint herbs into a tea. Mix one teaspoon of each and add just one teaspoon to a 6 ounce cup of hot water. Cover the cup, and steep for ten minutes.

When you are done for the day, try relaxing in your favorite chair or in your bed with a good book or listen to soothing music. You can also tense and relax different muscle groups starting with your face to help you relax before bed. Avoid drinking any drinks with caffeine in them at least four hours before bedtime. It takes four to six hours for caffeine to work through the system, and ingesting it too close to bedtime means that you will be up most of the night when all you really want is to sleep.

Chapter 5
Thyroid

Working our way down, we have the thyroid. This gland is located in your neck around where your Adam's apple would be if you are female. This gland works to regulate your metabolism to help you maintain a healthy weight and will release the hormones above when your exercising to help pump up your core body temperature, increasing your metabolism. This is the reason why you can walk from your gym to your car on a forty degree day not feel cold. Your body is wound up with hormones that are burning your fat at a higher than normal rate.

When your thyroid starts to get overtaxed, it can slow down making its hormones. This means you can have problems losing weight, be irritable, have bouts of depression, and trouble going to the bathroom among other things. This is a common problem, but it can be treatable. Not addressing this situation can lead to drastic measures, such as a removal of the thyroid, which means synthetic hormones for the rest of your life.

If your thyroid begins to overwork, you can have a condition called hyperthyroidism. This means that your body is constantly making the thyroid hormones. You may experience a hard time falling asleep, frequent trips to the bathroom, mood swings, rapid weight loss, and other symptoms. This can be a very serious condition.

There are a few essential oils you will have to add to the list above depending on which thyroid problem you're experiencing. Don't worry. There are two lists.

Hypothyroid Essential oils
Clove (Syzygium aromaticum)

Clove is employed to cleanse the thyroid and to help remove any blockages that may be causing the thyroid to function at lower levels.

Do not use if you are pregnant.

Lemongrass (Cymbopogon citratus)

This oil is listed here for its effectiveness in treating depression and anxiety.

Peppermint (Mentha piperita)

This oil can help combat the mental fatigue that one often has when their thyroid is working below normal levels. It helps to keep you alert.

Massage oil

- 2 Tablespoons Sweet Almond or Apricot Kernel Oil

- 5 Drops of Myrtle

- 2 Drops of Clove

- 2 Drops of lemongrass

- 3 drops of Peppermint

Mix all of this together. You can purchase a small bottle with a roller ball to place this oil blend into, but if you don't have one, you can store this in a small container. This blend needs to be massaged into the base of the neck on the spine and the on your big toes. You big toe is a reflexology point that is linked to your thyroid.

Diffuser Blend

- 2 Drops of Clove

- 3 drops of Myrtle

- 3 Drops of Sage

- 2 Drops of Lemongrass

Mix all of these together and place them on a diffuser pad and turn on the diffuser. You can also use a mug warmer. Just place the oils on the warmer before you plug it in.

Body butter

- 2 ounces of unscented Avocado Butter

- 1 Ounce of Shea Butter

- 10 Drops of Frankincense

- 10 Drops Myrtle

- 5 Drops Peppetmint

- 5 Drops Lemon Grass

- 5 Drops Sage

Blend the butters first. They need to be whipped on medium speed for 3 minutes. During this time, mix all of the oils together and then add them to the butters. You can purchase the butters in bulk online. You can also buy the dark glass container you need for this online as well. Once it is mixed, place it in the container and leave it overnight. When you're ready to use it, rub it into the base of the neck in the back, and work into the neck area where the thyroid is located.

To help bring your thyroid back up the normal levels, avoid GMO foods, over processed foods and caffeine. Add to your diet iodine rich foods like kelp and add a blue-green algae supplement.

Hyperthyroid Essential oils
Jasmine (Jaminum officinale)

Thought it is another one of the more expensive oils, it is instrumental in helping to balance out mood swings associated with hyperthyroidism. It's worth the investment. It's also good for taming the anxiety that comes with high levels of metabolic hormones.

Do not take if pregnant.

Juniper (juniperus communis)

This will detoxify the thyroid and calm nerves. It is also instrumental in preventing and treating cysts.

Do not take if pregnant.

Lemon Balm (Melissa officinalis)

This is an all-purpose essential oil for balancing emotions and preventing anxiety and depression.

Ylang-Ylang (Cananga odorata)

To combat the high pressure associated with hyperthyroidism, use this essential oil. It also helps to relieve stress ease anxiety, and will help you reach a calm state so you can sleep.

Massage Oil

- 2 Tablespoons of Sweet Almond or Apricot Kernel oil

- 2 drops of Juniper

- 4 Drops of Lemon Balm

- 2 Drops Ylang Ylang

- 2 Drops Virginian Cedarwood.

Mix all of the ingredients together and store in a small dark colored glass bottle. Massage into the base of the neck in back and on either side of the neck where the thyroid is located. Also massage into the big toe.

Diffuser Blend

- 2 Drops Clove

- 4 Drops Ylang-Ylang

- 4 Drops Lemon Balm

Mix all of them together and place on a diffuser pad or mug warmer. Can also be placed on a cotton ball and put in a heating vent.

Body Butter

- 2 Ounces of Avocado Butter

- 1 Ounce of Shea Butter

- 5 Drops Clove

- 10 Drops Myrtle

- 5 Drops Ylang-Ylang

- 5 Drops Sage

- 5 Drops Juniper

Mix the oils together. Whip the butter in a mixer for three minutes adding the oils as they mix. Store in a dark glass container overnight. Massage into the sie of the neck and the base of the neck in the back.

Emergency Shot

- 2 Drops of Ylang-Ylang

- 2 Drops of Geranium

- 4 Drops of Myrtle

- 2 Drops of Lemon Balm

Mix all of the oils. Place them in a zip lock bag. Throw in a cotton ball a make sure the cotton ball absorbs all of the oils. When you are feeling anxious, loose your temper or are highly nervous, open the bag and take a little whiff. You can carry this in your pocket or purse.

To help bring your thyroid back into balance, drink green juices, whole foods, food and herbs that are naturally capable of bringing down inflammation, like Basil, Oregano, and Rosemary. Add ginger to your cooking as well. Bone broth is another food to add to your regimen to help treat your thyroid.

Bone Broth

Place bones in a stock pot and cover with filtered water leaving enough room for the water to boil.

Add 2 tablespoons of Apple Cider Vinegar to extract the vitamins and minerals from the bone.

You can add vegetables for added flavor.

Bring to a boil and then allow to simmer, 24 hours for poultry bones, and up to 48 hours for beef and pork bones.

There will be a thick layer on top of the broth. Remove when you are ready to eat the broth.

You can also add stress relieving exercises and meditation to your daily routine as well. Deep breathing techniques can help you relax, calm, your nerves, and make it easier for you to sleep.

Deep Breathing

Sit in a comfortable position. Close your eyes. Take a slow breath in through your nose. This should take a slow count of at least six. As you do this, tighten a muscle group. It is best to start with the face and work your way down. As you slowly exhale to a count of eight, relax the muscle group. Inhale and tighten another muscle and exhale relaxing it. Do this until you have tensed and relaxed your feet and toes.

Chapter 6
The Pancreas

This gland plays an important role in the absorption and break down of the sugars you have every day. Every just about every type of grain, vegetable and fruit contains some type of sugar. We call the ones in grains and vegetables carbohydrates. The ones on fruits are called fructose. These sugars, unprocessed are turned into energy after the pancreas has released insulin into the system to break them down.

When the pancreas works overtime, it produces more insulin that is needed, and the adrenal glands release cortisol to try to counteract it. This is hypoglycemia. If you constantly eat foods that have refined sugars in them or any highly processed grains, your pancreas tries to work fast in assimilating the sugar you put in your system. This taxes the gland and can lead it overproducing insulin. This leads to confusion, inability to concentrate, fainting spells, headaches and many other dangerous side effects.

The best course of action is to remove all refined sugars from the diet. This will allows the pancreas to return to normal function. Also drop the white bread and go for whole grain. Much like Diabetes, break up your meals into small ones throughout the day. Carry whole grain crackers with peanut butter for when you overdo it and you start to feel woozy. Passing out doesn't happen immediately. You just feel really tired and unable to keep your eyes open.

Essential oils for the pancreas
Corriander (Coriandum sativum)

This essential oil has been used to help awaken cells and promote healing.

Eucalyptus, Blue gum (Eucalyptus globulus)

This essential oil has been clinically proven to help rebuild pancreatic beta cells. This means it can effectively treat diabetes.

Fennel (Foeniculum vulgare)

This is another essential oil whose lab tests have proven that helps to stimulate cell growth in the pancreas. It has also been discovered to stimulate the production of insulin.

Ocotea (ocotea quixos)

Even though this oil is relatively new to the scene, it has already proven its worth in the treatment of diabetes by being a forerunner in helping normalize blood glucose levels.

Massage oil for Diabetes

- 2 Tablespoons of Sweet Almond Oil or Apricot Kernel Oil

- 2 Drops Ocotea oil

- 4 Drops Fennel oil

- 3 Drops Eucalyptus Oil

- 3 Drops Sage

Mix all of the oils together and massage in clock-wise circles where the pancreas is located. Also massage a small point on the left palm directly next to the pinky knuckle.

Diffuser Blend

- 2 Drops Coriander Oil

- 4 Drops Fennel Oil

- 2 Drops Eucalyptus Oil

- 2 Drops Juniper Oil

Mix all oils together and then apply to a diffuser or mug warmer. If you don't have either, you can use a lightbulb, but please, apply the oils before you turn on the lamp and keep an eye on it.

Chapter 7
Your Kidneys

Your kidneys are as much a vital part of the endocrine system as your other glands. They release adrenaline to give you an extra boost when you need and cortisol when you need to cope with stress. They produce more than 30 hormones in total.

When your kidneys are taxed, you feel run down, irritable, sleepy, and have mood swings that rival those of the reproductive organs. They can produce more cortisol when they are not in balance as well, leading to confusion, an compromised immune system and other serious conditions.

If you have been diagnosed as having Kidney Fatigue, steer clear of sugars, caffeine, alcohol and other mood changing substances. Your kidneys need a break. You have to place yourself in a less stressful environment to allow your kidneys time to heal and reset.

The trick to doing this is to use essential oils that boost mental acuity, energy levels and balance emotions. This will take the extra weight off of the kidneys and allow them rest, and heal. This best part is, that if you have been getting the ones above, you won't have to add to your list.

Massage Oil

- 2 Ounces of Sweet Almond or Apricot Kernel Oil

- 5 drops of Juniper

- 5 Drops of Ylang-Ylang

- 10 Drops of Peppermint

- 5 Drops of Myrtle

Mix together and store in a dark glass container with a tight lid. Massage a small amount in clock-wise circles both in front where your kidneys are located and on your back as well. Do this three times daily

Stimulating Diffuser Oil

- 5 Drops Juniper

- 5 Drops Peppermint

Mix and place in a diffuser or mug warmer. This blend will permeate a large bedroom and last for a few hours. You can also place this blend in a plastic bag with a cotton ball and sniff when you need a pick-me-up.

Stress Busting Blend

- 2 Drops of Lavender

- 2 Drops of Geranium

- 2 Drops of Ylang-Ylang

- 4 Drops of Sage

Mix and place in a diffuser or mug/candle warmer. This will help you relax from the day's stressors, and allow you to drift off to sleep.

Mineral Bath

- 1/2 of fine Sea Salt

- 1/4 Cup of Borax

- 1/4 Cup Baking soda

- 2 Tablespoons Sweet Almond or Apricot Kernel Oil

- 10 Drops Juniper

- 10 Drops Peppermint

- 10 Drops Lavender

- 5 Drops Myrtle

- 5 Drops Frankincense

Mix all the dry ingredients first. Then mix all of the oils. Pour the dry into the oils and mix thoroughly. Place in an air tight container overnight. To use, pour 1/4 cup into warm running water, soak and enjoy.

Chapter 8
Your Reproductive Glands

As we age our reproductive organs start to slow down production of the hormones that allow us procreate. This means less estrogen for the ladies and less testosterone for the males. There is hope and things that you can do to keep your sex drive up, your hormones level, and your emotions on an even keel.

For The Women

There are those of us that look forward to not having to worry about sanitary napkins, tampons or the other things we use during our monthly cycle. What we don't look forward to is to is the restless sleep, night sweats, hot flashes, and becoming a little scatter-brained, all symptoms of perimenopause and menopause.

Perimenopause can start as early as in our thirties to get us ready for when we stop having periods. This means our periods become erratic and hard to track. This also means moods swings, uncontrollable crying, and weight fluctuations that can drive you up a wall.

You can use apps like Fertility Friend to effectively track when you're spotting, when you flow and the heaviness of it, and all the symptoms you are experiencing in the interim. There are others out there, but this one is highly recommended.

Our bodies start producing less estrogen. This can lead lighter periods, irritability, sleeplessness, and mood swings. This can also lead to intermittent hot flashes as well. Here are a couple of oils to add to your list:

Basil (Ocimum basilicum)

This is an oil that will become one of your best friends. In blends it helps with concentration, mental and physical fatigue. It can help to balance your moods and even help with menstrual cramps

Cypress (Cupressus sempervirens)

This can help relieve water retention, prevent hot flashes, sweating and being irritable.

Night Massage Oil

- 3 Ounces of Sweet Almond or Apricot Kernel Oil'

- 1/2 Ounce of Grapeseed oil

- 1/2 Ounce Avocado oil

- 15 Drops of Basil

- 10 Drops of Roman Chamomile (Natural Estrogen)

- 5 Drops of Clary Sage (From above, for hot flashes, sweats, and trouble sleeping.)

- 10 Drops of Cypress

- 5 Drops of Geranium

- 5 Drops of Peppermint

Mix all of them together and place in a dark colored glass bottle with a tight lid. Massage clock-wise into the abdomen area before bed.

Mood Diffuser

- 2 Drops Roman Chamomile

- 2 Drops Clary Sage

- 2 Drops Geranium

- 4 Drops Cypress

Mix all of them together and place in a diffuser or mug/candle warmer. Basil is not used in this blend because of its stimulating effect.

Concentration Blend

- 3 Drops Basil

- 7 Drops Peppermint

Mix together and place in either a perfume bottle or a plastic bag with a cotton ball. When you are having trouble maintaining your concentration, simply take a light sniff and let the oils do the rest.

For the Men

Many men don't want to admit it, but when they get older, they lose a step. Low testosterone can cause muscle loss, fatigue, and lack of desire in the bedroom. You just need add one more to the list:

Yarrow (Achillea millefolium)

This promotes healthy glandular function and helps to increase the testosterone in the body.

Massage Oil

- 4 Ounces of Sweet Almond or Apricot Kernel Oil

- 10 Drops of Fennel

- 10 Drops of Yarrow

- 5 Drops of Sage

- 10 Drops of myrtle

- 15 Drops of Cypress

Mix all the ingredients together in a dark glass container. Massage into the base of the skull in the back and also in the joints around the entire groin area.

You can also make this combination without the carrier oils (the first ingredients) and place ten drops in a diffuser or on a mug/candle warmer.

You can also mix three drops of the blend into a tablespoon of a liquid soap and wash yourself as normal, avoid the eyes and other sensitive areas.

Conclusion

I hope this book will help you on your way to glandular and hormone health. Remember to listen to your body. It has way of telling if you are on the right track. By eating right, exercising, and avoiding high-stress situations, you can aid your body's natural healing processes, and in so doing bring your life back into balance as well.

Steer clear of ingredients in food you cannot pronounce or that you don't think should be in your food. Stay away from GMO and artificial additives as well. The closer you stay to the food being in its natural state, the better you will feel in the long run.

Exercise can be as simple as taking a walk or as involved as taking classes in a gym. Relieving stress can be done with Yoga or simple meditation techniques. It's your body, and it will tell you what to do and what to avoid.

I recommended two different carrier oils for those who have nut allergies. As for the avocado and grapeseed oils, they will your skin stay soft and smooth during your life transition as our skin tends to become dry.

Resources:

http://www.webmd.com/sleep-disorders/tc/melatonin-overview

healthywomen.org

webmd.com

http://www.hormone.org/hormones-and-health/the-endocrine-system/endocrine-glands-and-types-of-hormones#Thyroid

http://www.endocrineweb.com/conditions/thyroid/how-your-thyroid-works

http://www.wakingtimes.com/2014/10/22/treating-pineal-gland-essential-oils/

http://www.trueactivist.com/how-to-de-calcify-your-pineal-gland-with-food/

https://www.organicfacts.net/health-benefits/essential-oils/myrtle-essential-oil.html

http://www.sigmaaldrich.com/life-science/nutrition-research/learning-center/plant-profiler/foeniculum-vulgare.html

http://www.quinessence.com/blog/essential-oils-for-menopause

https://movableqi.wordpress.com/2012/06/04/young-living-essential-oils-and-mens-health-wellness/

www.ingramcontent.com/pod-product-compliance
Lightning Source LLC
Chambersburg PA
CBHW062053280526
45788CB00003B/1211